The Small Ecological Garden

Sue Stickland

SEARCH PRESS / HDRA

First published in Great Britain 1996

Search Press Limited
Wellwood, North Farm Road,
Tunbridge Wells, Kent TN2 3DR

in association with

The Henry Doubleday Research Association
National Centre for Organic Gardening
Ryton-on-Dunsmore
Coventry CV8 3LG

ISBN 0 85532 773 1

Printed in Spain by A.G. Elkar S. Coop, 48012 Bilbao

Contents

Introduction

Ecological gardening means working with nature and without chemicals. It means getting to know your garden – its soil, aspect and climate – so you can choose plants which naturally suit it and create conditions where they will thrive. Plant debris and other organic 'waste' are returned to the soil by making compost and leafmould and using mulches. This provides food for soil-living creatures, and their activities in turn release nutrients for new plant growth – just as would happen in nature. Plants which have the right conditions and the right diet are healthy, and less prone to pest and disease attacks.

Wildlife is encouraged into the ecological garden by providing a variety of habitats and plentiful sources of food. In a garden with a flourishing wildlife community, each creature has its enemies and a natural balance will be established. This makes it less likely that any one creature will get out of hand and become a pest. Good habitats include a pond, a hedge, a dry-stone wall, or more simply a pile of logs left to rot in an odd corner. Plants which supply nectar, pollen, seeds or berries are all good food sources. Some native plants should be used where appropriate – in hedges and wildflower 'meadows', for example – as these tend to encourage a greater range of wildlife than exotic species.

Bringing in wildlife does not mean that an ecological garden has to be a wilderness. It should be a place for people as well – somewhere attractive to the eye and soothing to the spirit. These aims need not conflict. A drift of wild flowers in a corner can look wonderful

and will also provide food and shelter for wild-life. Nor need an ecological garden be large or in the depths of the country – it can equally well be a small plot in the middle of town.

Whatever its size or location, your garden can make an important contribution to the natural world. While buildings, factories, roads and modern farming methods are destroying habitats for wildlife, gardens can provide safe havens for some of the creatures and plants which have been displaced. The effect can be significant, since the total area of domestic gardens in the U.K. is greater than that covered by the country's nature reserves.

Another important contribution can be made by composting. Of the total domestic rubbish collected by local authorities, a large proportion is 'green' waste. By recycling your garden and kitchen waste, you can avoid the pollution caused by taking it to landfill sites. And finally, as a result of all your efforts, you may enjoy being in your garden so much that you do not need to get in the car and drive to the country!

This book is too short to deal with gardening techniques, particularly the specialised organic methods for growing fruit and vegetables, but there are many other books that can help you (see page 47). The book aims to help you with the basics of an ecological garden – to help you create a framework of plants and wildlife habitats, and a composting system which will allow you to enjoy an interesting and attractive garden while still maintaining a harmonious relationship with the natural world.

Planning an ecological garden

Before making any changes to your garden, it is important to find out as much about it as possible. Note down:

• which way it faces and whether it slopes
• the pattern of sun and shade
• the direction of the prevailing wind
• the amount and pattern of rainfall
• places where it is particularly wet or particularly dry
• likely maximum and minimum temperatures
• likely dates of the first and last frosts
• the type and depth of the soil (see pages 12–15).

Although you could get a few of these facts from the local weather station and neighbouring gardeners, most are unique to your garden. To find these things out, you will need to observe your garden closely throughout the year and become in tune with it from season to season.

These factors affect not only what plants you can grow and where you put them, but also the siting of other features such as the lawn, or the pond, or even the compost heap. In an ecological garden, giving everything the right conditions helps solve problems before they arise.

Creating microclimates

Many of the conditions in your garden will necessarily be determined by its geographical location, but you can sometimes modify them, perhaps just in small areas of the garden, to give a better 'microclimate' for your plants.

One of the most effective ways of doing this is to use walls, hedges, fences and other windbreaks, both surrounding and within the garden (see page 8). Wind causes physical damage and stunts plant growth, and also exacerbates the effects of cold; so reducing its influence makes the garden a pleasanter place for you as well as for your plants.

Although you cannot make it rain, you can prepare for drought by applying mulches to retain moisture in the soil (see pages 37–38) and by using water more efficiently (see page 44). In high-rainfall areas, you can use raised beds to increase the drainage in small areas of the garden. This will help make them suitable for plants such as thyme, lavender and other shrubby herbs that do not like wet feet.

Choosing plants

Suitable conditions   In an ecological garden, it is important to choose plants with the growing conditions in mind. If sun-loving plants are put in the shade, or moisture-loving plants are put in dry conditions, they will never thrive. Not only will they look less attractive, but also the stress they are under will make them more susceptible to attack by pests and diseases.

Attractive all year round   In a small garden plants must look good for as long as possible: there is little scope for disguising dead leaves and straggly growth. Choose herbaceous plants with leaves or seedheads which remain attractive after the flowers have faded, and shrubs with a long flowering period or eye-catching berries, foliage or bark.

Resistance to pests and diseases   However good the conditions, there are some plants which are particularly susceptible to pests and diseases. Hostas, for example, seem to attract slugs from miles around! The best solution may be not to grow such plants at all – there are usually good alternatives. Sometimes specific varieties of common plants show resistance to disease: roses that are less susceptible to black spot or mildew, for example. Look out for these in seed and nursery catalogues.

Attractive to wildlife   If possible, choose plants that provide food for wildlife (see pages 26–31).

Buying plants

Garden centres only sell a limited range of plants, so it is worth going to a specialist nursery to get exactly what you want: plants for particular conditions or dwarf forms of herbaceous perennials, for example. For native hedging plants, try nurseries that supply hedging contractors, or contact local conservation groups.

Do not be tempted to accept plants from friends and neighbours unless you are sure that they are free from pests and diseases: it is easier to avoid problems than to get rid of them once they are in the garden.

Planning an ecological garden

You can see the importance of getting things in the right place

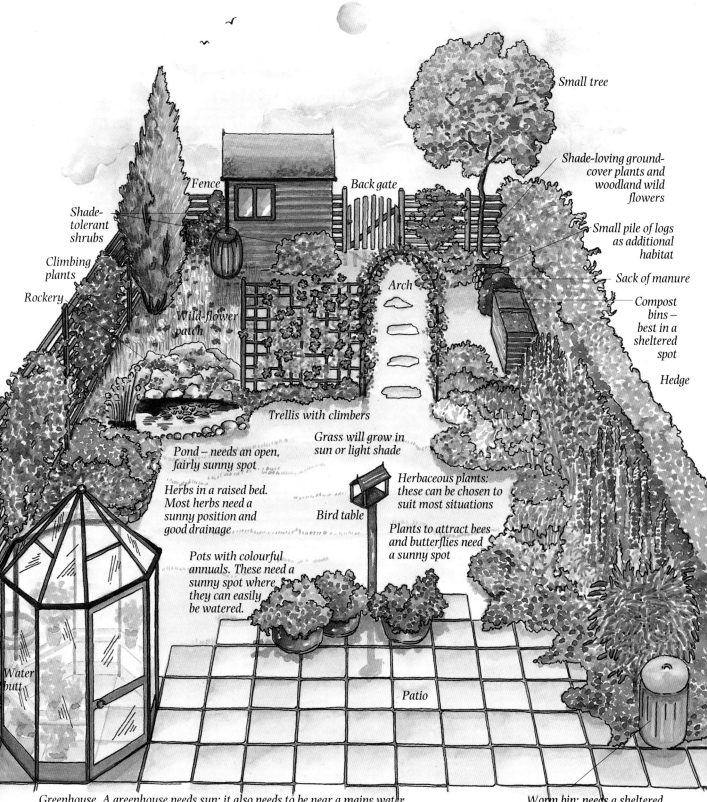

Small tree

Shade-loving ground-cover plants and woodland wild flowers

Fence

Back gate

Shade-tolerant shrubs

Small pile of logs as additional habitat

Climbing plants

Sack of manure

Rockery

Arch

Compost bins – best in a sheltered spot

Wild-flower patch

Hedge

Trellis with climbers

Pond – needs an open, fairly sunny spot

Grass will grow in sun or light shade

Herbs in a raised bed. Most herbs need a sunny position and good drainage

Herbaceous plants: these can be chosen to suit most situations

Bird table

Plants to attract bees and butterflies need a sunny spot

Pots with colourful annuals. These need a sunny spot where they can easily be watered.

Water butt

Patio

Greenhouse. A greenhouse needs sun; it also needs to be near a mains water supply and, if possible, an electricity supply

Worm bin: needs a sheltered spot, shady in summer

7

Using boundaries

One of the most effective ways of modifying conditions within the garden is to use walls, hedges, fences and other windbreaks. As well as providing shelter, these give privacy and make a barrier against noise and dust. Hedges, and climbing plants against walls and fences, can also provide shelter and food for wildlife.

The best windbreak effect is provided by those barriers that filter rather than block the wind; ideally they should be about 50 per cent holes. Solid walls and fences and very dense hedges can cause damaging eddies on their leeward side. On a sloping site they can also trap cold air and create frost pockets.

Hedges, walls and fences will give shelter over a distance of about six to eight times their height, so one that is 1.5–1.8m (5–6ft) tall round the boundary of a small garden gives it good protection.

Localised shelter

You can also use extra localised shelter; for example

• a trellis of sweet peas to protect a seating area in summer, or an evergreen shrub to bring on delicate spring bulbs.

• small movable windbreaks to protect plants at times when they are most vulnerable: newly planted shrubs during a cold winter spell, for example. These can be made of windbreak netting or of woven hurdles.

A trellis of climbers is useful for shelter and screening within the garden.

Fences

Fences provide cheap instant windbreaks. Try to ensure that there are either horizontal or vertical gaps between the slats to filter the wind. This may be easier to do if you make up the fence yourself rather than

Hurdles are woven from natural hazel or willow stems and make good windbreaks.

This fence has gaps in it to filter the wind and avoid turbulence.

Climbing plants such as this clematis need the support of wires or netting fastened to the wall.

Clothe your walls in living colour with this purple ivy; it will cling to the wall without support.

buying off-the-peg panels. Train climbing plants on a latticework of wires set about 8–10cm (3–4in) out from the fence; a few ledges set behind the green curtain make ideal nesting sites for some garden birds.

Walls

Walls and fences take up less space than a hedge, and this can be an advantage in a small garden. Walls also hold the heat, hence modifying the temperature close by. Those that face south and west create warm sheltered spots which are ideal for tender plants.

Hedges

Hedges provide food, shelter and first-class nesting sites for birds, and they act as sheltered corridors for creatures going from garden to garden and to wild areas beyond. They can also be an attractive feature in the garden, whether you choose a flowering hedge such as *Rosa rugosa* with its long-lasting blooms and large red hips (see page 27), or a simple clipped evergreen such as holly.

Holly can be clipped into a neat evergreen hedge, with the additional interest of berries in winter.

Alternatively, you could plant a mixed hedge of wild shrub and tree species (see pages 10–11). Be wary of conifers as some species are not suitable for hedges in small gardens.

You need to allow a strip about a metre (a yard) wide for planting most hedges and then a further metre/yard between the hedge and fruit or vegetables, or moisture-loving flowers. Most formally clipped hedges need an annual trim in late summer. Informal flowering hedges need only a light prune to stop them becoming straggly. Wait until winter when the berries have gone. Never clip a hedge in the nesting season.

A mixed hedge For maximum value to wildlife, combined with beauty and interest all year round, plant a mixed hedge of wild shrubs and trees. These can be clipped into a dense tidy hedge which will not be out of place in a small garden. Choose one main species as a basis for the hedge; hawthorn, blackthorn or field maple are good choices. Mix in about twenty per cent of other species, choosing some evergreens to provide winter cover. Many of the species produce flowers and berries, but you will only see them at their best if you clip parts of the hedge every other year instead of annually.

Acer campestre field maple – a suitable base tree for a mixed hedge.

Cornus sanguinea dogwood – an easy-to-grow shrub, enhanced by coloured stems in winter.

Crataegus monogyna hawthorn. Fragrant white flowers in spring and haws the birds will love in the autumn.

Ligustrum vulgare – wild privet – has scented white flowers in the summer.

Euonymus europaeus spindle. This does well on alkaline soils. Birds love the seeds.

Prunus spinosa blackthorn. A haze of white flowers in the spring and bluish-black sloes in autumn.

Rhamnus catharticus buckthorn – the food plant of the caterpillar of the brimstone butterfly. It also eats *Rhamnus frangula* alder buckthorn.

Quercus spp. oak. The oak is home to birds and also to numerous species of creepy-crawlies at the bottom of the food chain.

Ilex aquifolium holly. White flowers in spring, and in winter the familiar bright red berries to feed the birds.

Fagus sylvestris beech – a tree with stunning autumn colour. The leaves stay on the tree all winter.

Viburnum opulus guelder rose. White flowers in summer and vibrantly coloured berries and foliage in autumn.

Corylus avellana hazel. Catkins, then hazelnuts; harvest some for yourself and leave some for the voles.

Looking at your soil

The living world beneath the surface of the garden concerns the ecological gardener just as much as the more visible one above. It is important to get conditions right for the many inhabitants of the soil, from earthworms to microscopic bacteria and fungi, as they are responsible for supplying food to your plants. It is also important that plant roots should be able to penetrate the soil easily in order to obtain food and moisture. Study your soil closely, and find out how you can improve it.

What does it feel like?

Rub some topsoil between your fingers. A soil that is predominantly sand feels gritty; silt feels smooth; and clay feels sticky. Other types of soil include spongy black peaty soils and chalky soils. The type of soil you have influences what you can do to improve it and, to some extent, which plants will grow well (see pages 14–15).

Testing your soil type and structure by rubbing some topsoil between your fingers.

Now crush a clod of soil in your hand. Ideally it should be friable whether it is wet or dry, indicating that it has a good structure.

A well-structured soil drains well and lets in air, yet still holds reserves of water: good conditions for soil life and plant roots. Poorly structured soil tends to be hard and dusty when dry, and sticky when wet.

To improve the soil structure   Add organic matter, use mulches, and keep cultivation to a minimum.

What does it look like?

Look down any holes that you dig, particularly deep ones for fence posts or pipes, and observe the different layers in the soil (its 'profile'). Ideally, you should see a deep layer of dark topsoil over a light subsoil and no hard compacted layers. The topsoil should contain plenty of earthworm burrows and long branching plant roots.

To improve compacted soils   Dig and add organic matter.

To improve shallow soils   Build them up gradually with organic matter; meanwhile, make extensive planting holes for trees and shrubs. If water sits in the bottom of a hole and stays there for a few days, this is a sign that land drains may be necessary.

What plants are growing?

You can tell a lot about a soil's fertility from the way the plants are growing. Even a crop of weeds can sometimes be a good sign!

Vigorous clumps of chickweed at least indicate that the soil is fertile.

The type of plants in the garden or surrounding area can also indicate whether the soil is acid or alkaline (see page 13). In an established ecological garden where compost and other organic materials are regularly used, plants should be able to obtain nearly all the nutrients they need from the soil. Initially, however, you may need to add organic fertilisers to correct deficiencies and to feed the plants while the soil fertility builds up.

If plant growth is poor for no obvious reason   it is worth sending away a soil sample for professional analysis – preferably to a service designed specifically for organic growers.

Soil acidity

The acidity or alkalinity of the soil is measured by its pH. It is worth getting an accurate value of this by using a testing kit (available from most garden centres) or by sending a sample away for analysis. The pH may vary across the garden if different areas have had different treatment in the past. For example, a vegetable plot may have been limed (possibly over-limed).

The soil pH should ideally be around 6.0–6.5, although most plants will tolerate levels between 5.5 and 7.0. Outside this range, the ability of the soil to provide nutrients for plants will be affected.

To make soils less acid   Add ground limestone, dolomite, or calcified seaweed.

To make soils less alkaline   This is more difficult to correct, but constant addition of compost and manure should gradually help.

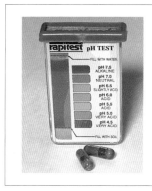

Soil testing kit. There are various types, so follow the manufacturers' instructions.

Pieris (above), *Rhododendron* spp. azalea (top) and *Rhododendron* spp. rhododendron (left): if you see these plants growing in your garden, it is a good indication that the soil is acid.

Soil types

Clay and silty soils

Sandy soil

Clay soils are difficult to work, particularly when wet or very dry, and they are slow to drain, hence slow to warm up in spring. However, they usually contain a rich supply of nutrients.

   Silty soils can similarly be wet and cold, and are easily compacted. They may not be so fertile as clays. To improve both clay and silty soils, add organic matter to help drainage and to make the soil easier for plant roots to penetrate. Avoid over-cultivation.

Roses thrive on clay and silty soil. Try also *Mahonia* (see page 23), *Cornus* dogwood (see page 10), *Helleborus* hellebores, *Hedera* ivy (see page 9), *Corylus* hazel (see page 11), *Primula*, and *Hemerocallis* day lily.

Sandy soils are light and easy to work. They drain freely and therefore warm up quickly in spring. However, this means that they can be prone to drought, and that nutrients and lime are easily washed out. Keep adding organic matter to hold water and supply nutrients. Use mulches where possible, and avoid turning over the soil, as this speeds up loss of water and organic matter. Check the pH annually and add lime if the soil has become too acid.

Aubrieta likes a well-drained sandy soil, as do *Fagus* beech (see page 11), *Artemisia*, *Cistus* rock rose, *Philadelphus* (see page 21), *Achillea* yarrow, and *Lychnis* campion.

Chalky soil

Peaty soil

Chalky soils often have a thin topsoil which drains easily. They are therefore prone to drought and lose nutrients easily. Chalky soils are also very alkaline, which can make it difficult for plants to take up certain nutrients. Add organic matter to build up the depth of the soil, retain moisture and provide nutrients. Use mulches where possible. Organic matter should also help reduce the alkalinity of the soil.

Peaty soils are dark and spongy, and rich in organic matter. They tend to get waterlogged and are usually very acid. Large quantities of additional organic matter are not necessary for improving these soils. Put in land drains if need be to prevent waterlogging, or grow plants that need good drainage in raised beds. Check the pH, and add lime where required to make the soil less acid.

Pinks flourish in chalky soil. Other suitable plants would be *Syringa* lilac, *Lathyrus* sweet pea, *Spiraea*, *Aquilegia* columbine, *Buddleia* (see page 28), *Primula* and clematis.

Lime-hating plants such as camellias do well on peaty soils, providing they are well drained, as do *Gaultheria*, *Gentiana* gentian, most heathers (see page 22), *Pieris* (see page 13) and *Rhododendron* (see page 13).

Feeding the soil

Supplying the soil with bulky organic materials such as compost, manures and leaf-mould is an essential part of ecological gardening. They improve the soil structure, encourage a healthy population of soil-living creatures, and help provide a steady balanced supply of plant foods.

Many of these organic materials can come from recycling within the garden itself. If you put kitchen waste in the dustbin and burn the leaves that fall in your drive, you are not only throwing away your soil's fertility, but also adding to problems at local rubbish tips and to the pollution of the atmosphere.

Just as nature eventually returns to the soil every plant that dies and leaf that falls, so you too should value every bit of organic matter that comes your way. Unlike in nature, however, recycling in a small garden needs helping along.

Newspaper, cardboard and leaves
Small amounts of these can be added.

Torn-up newspaper. Avoid using glossy paper printed in colour

Autumn leaves

Stemmy materials will bulk up and aerate the heap.

Weeds – but not the roots of pernicious weeds (see page 36–37) – and debris from beds and borders

Chopped-up stemmy material such as hedge-clippings

Straw and/or hay – you should chop this up before adding it to the heap

How to make a compost heap
Make sure you have a mixture of bulky, stemmy materials and soft, sappy materials in the heap. Mix them up well; water the ingredients if they are dry; and cover them to keep in heat and moisture.

Making compost

Any pile of garden and kitchen waste will make compost of a sort eventually. However, you can make better compost more quickly if you choose the ingredients with care (see the illustration below) and if you use a compost bin (see page 19). Turning and mixing the materials at least once while they are composting also speeds up the process.

The best site for a compost heap or bin is somewhere warm and sheltered, and preferably easily accessible with a wheelbarrow. Liquid needs to be able to run out of the compost, so you should either site the heap or bin on soil or, if it is on a hard surface, make some provision for drainage.

The finished compost is invaluable both for improving the soil structure and as a balanced source of nutrients for plants.

Shredding

A shredder which chops up woody materials allows you to recycle garden waste such as prunings and hedge clippings. Small amounts of this shredded material can be added to the compost heap; the rest makes a useful mulch for shrubberies and paths. Avoid using woody shreddings where they would get dug into the soil, as they can temporarily deplete it of nitrogen.

Allow space for storing a separate pile of material for shredding. Electric shredders need to be near a power supply, but are rather quieter than those with petrol motors.

Electric shredder.

Kitchen waste

Kitchen scraps such as vegetable peelings – avoid meat or fish scraps unless you have a rat-proof bin

Soft and sappy materials

are 'activators' – they will heat up the heap and get it going.

Young nettles

Manures

Grass cuttings

Do not use

Manures from intensive livestock systems such as battery chickens and pigs; rubbish such as metal, plastic or glass; and cat and dog waste.

Worm bins

A worm bin is ideal for composting small amounts of materials – daily kitchen waste, or the debris from a tiny garden. Manure worms or 'brandlings' eat their way through it and produce 'worm compost'. This is a valuable product, rich in plant nutrients.

You can set up a worm bin in any container, provided that it has good drainage and keeps the material inside moist and the rain out. A plastic dustbin drilled with holes will do, or buy one of the purpose-built worm bins on the market. The bin should be kept in a sheltered spot, out of full sun in summer, and ideally in a porch or garden shed in winter.

Worm compost is particularly useful for putting in potting mixtures and for top-dressing plants in pots. A worm bin is therefore worth having even when ordinary compost heaps are necessary as well.

Brandling worms. These are distinguishable from earthworms by the noticeable bands round their bodies.

Worm bin

Water the surface if the mixture gets dry

Worms like to be warm, so keep the bin out of cold winds and frost

Drill holes near the bottom to let water escape

Put a lid on the bin to keep flies out

Cover the waste with newspaper to prevent any smell

Add a little chopped waste every day (not meat or orange peel)

Put the worms in some leaf mould or strawy manure

Place a board with some small holes in it on to the gravel

Put some gravel in the bottom

Leaf-mould

Small amounts of autumn leaves can be added to a compost heap, but if you can collect more it is worth making leaf-mould. Almost any kind of container will do for this – plastic sacks for small amounts or simple wire-netting enclosures (see the picture below) for larger quantities. Just fill the containers full of moist leaves. In one or two years they will have rotted enough to use on the garden.

Leaf-mould supplies few plant foods, but is invalu-able for improving the soil structure. You can use it liberally where adding lots of nutrients is un-necessary or undesirable: on annual flowers and seedbeds, for example. Let the leaves remain in the bin for another year, and they will give you a fine crumbly product which makes an excel-lent substitute for peat in potting composts.

Manure and other brought-in materials

If you need extra organic material for the garden, strawy farmyard or stable manure is often one of the easiest to obtain. Small amounts can be added to the compost bin. Stack larger amounts in plastic sacks or under polythene until it rots. This prevents the nitrogen it contains from being washed out, and also gives any chemical residues a chance to break down. The nutrients (particularly nitrogen) it contains are more readily available to plants than those in compost, and are more easily leached from the soil. Use it in moderation, reserving it for particularly hungry plants such as roses.

Other organic materials that you might bring into the garden include hay, straw, seaweed, bark and woodchips.

Comfrey is often grown by organic gardeners as a compost activator or fertiliser, used as a mulch, or made into a liquid feed for plants. If your garden is big enough, why not try growing a patch?

Compost bins

Compost bins help the compost-making process by:

• keeping the material tidy;

• keeping the heat in, hence speeding up the decomposition;

• keeping rain out, preventing waterlogging and stopping nutrients washing out.

Small bins in particular need to be well insulated: the smaller the volume, the greater the amount of heat that is likely to be lost through the sides. If your own garden does not produce much compost material, one answer is to bring in more so you can fill a bigger bin.

You can easily lift off some bins from the heap when they are full. This makes it easy to turn the materials and to start a new heap.

A bin should have a lid to keep water out and heat in

There should be no wide gaps in the sides which let heat out

If you are buying a proprietary compost bin, make sure that it is made of a good insulating material. This one is plastic.

A home-made bin made of wood. Put a piece of carpet on top of the material to keep the heat in.

Home-made compost bin built out of wire and carpet.

Compost tumbler: all you do is turn the tumbler on its frame once a day. This eliminates having to turn and layer a compost heap.

Plants for different conditions

A plant will only thrive if it has the right growing conditions. The type of soil can be important (see pages 12–15) and so can the site – whether it is sunny or shady, dry or moist, windy or sheltered.

Before buying any new plant, find out what conditions it needs and make sure that it is suitable for your garden. Sometimes it helps to know where similar plants grow in the wild. Shrubby herbs such as thyme and lavender, for example, which grow freely on rocky slopes in the Mediterranean, will not like a cold, heavy soil.

There are plants which grow well in all sorts of extreme conditions, as nature well illustrates. Think of the sundew that sits in a wet acid peat bog, for example, or the sea holly that grows out of shingle on the beach.

Conditions in the garden are unlikely to be severe, but plants which tolerate relatively tough conditions are still useful, particularly where the prime sites in the garden are occupied by fruit and vegetables. The following pages give some appropriate suggestions.

Plants will flourish best in the conditions they are naturally suited to: bear this in mind when choosing them.

Hot dry areas

There are many plants suitable for these conditions; a few of them are shown on this page.

◀ *Alyssum* spp. alyssum.

Other suitable plants would be:
Allium spp. ornamental onions
Achillea spp. yarrow
Foeniculum vulgare fennel (see page 30)
Gypsophila repens gypsophila
Mesembryanthemum criniflorum Livingstone daisy
Nepeta mussinii catmint
Santolina spp. cotton lavender

▲ *Sedum* spp. sedum. Bees and other insects love this plant.

◀ *Philadelphus* spp. mock orange.

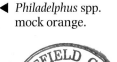

▲ *Ceanothus* spp. ceanothus. Another suitable climber would be *Jasminum officinale* summer jasmine.

▶ *Salvia officinalis* sage.

Some other good trees and shrubs to plant:
Artemisia spp. artemisia
Buddleia spp. butterfly bush (see page 28)
Cistus spp. rock rose
Helianthemum spp. helianthemum
Lavandula spp. lavender
Thymus spp. thyme (see page 29)

Rosmarinus officinalis *rosemary.* ▶

Windy areas

Certain plants tolerate wind better than others: choose tough plants like the ones suggested on this page. In general, plants suitable for seaside areas are also likely to be suitable, but may not be frost-hardy.

▶ *Eryngium* spp. sea holly.

Other good plants for windy areas:
Achillea spp. yarrow
Alyssum spp. alyssum (see page 21)
Astrantia major astrantia
Santolina spp. cotton lavender
Sedum spectabile ice plant

Alchemilla mollis lady's mantle. ▶

◀ *Jasminum officinale* summer jasmine.

Some other suitable climbers:
Clematis macropetala clematis (see page 9)
Jasminum nudiflorum winter jasmine (see page 23)

▲ *Clematis montana* clematis – a fast-growing, vigorous climber.

The following trees and shrubs are also wind-resistant:
Calluna spp. heather
Cistus spp. rock rose
Cotoneaster spp. cotoneaster
Crataegus monogyna hawthorn (see page 10)
Hippophae rhamnoides sea buckthorn
Ilex aquifolium holly (see page 11)

▲ *Pyracantha* spp. pyracantha.

◀ *Erica* spp. heather – a good ground-cover plant.

Dry shade

Dry shade is always a problem area, but if you choose the right plants you will find that even here you can have a useful splash of colour.

◀ Try naturalising *Cyclamen hederifolium* under trees.

These plants are also suitable for dry shade
Bergenia spp. bergenia
Dicentra eximia dicentra
Epimedium spp. epimedium
Geranium macrorrhizum cranesbill
Helleborus foetidus stinking hellebore
Heuchera sanguina heuchera
Lunaria annua honesty (see page 28)

▲ *Jasminum nudiflorum* winter jasmine.

Other climbers for this location:
Hedera helix ivy (see page 9)
Hydrangea petiolaris climbing hydrangea

▲ *Vinca minor* periwinkle.

▼ *Symphoricarpus x doorenbossii* snowberry.

◀ *Mahonia aquifolium* mahonia.

Some other suitable trees and shrubs:
Pyracantha spp. pyracantha (see page 22)
Skimmia japonica skimmia

Hedgehogs find shelter in log-piles and neglected corners of the garden and like to hibernate in the dry leaves beneath a hedge...

... and they prey on your slugs.

Slow-worms are harmless – except to slugs!

Creating habitats for wildlife

This may sound like creating a nature reserve, but in fact any garden is home to a whole host of creatures, from spiders, insects and other creepy-crawlies to birds and small mammals. There is no need for major changes. By sympathetic planting and management, and perhaps by introducing a few extra features to the garden, you can encourage the build-up of this natural community.

The worst possible garden for wildlife is one that is all lawn, all vegetables, or all roses. The more diverse it is, with different plants and different features, the more habitats are created and the more different creatures it is likely to attract.

In the garden borders, try to develop several layers of vegetation – a tree if you have room, a lower canopy of shrubs, and shade-loving plants beneath. Include some evergreens for winter cover, and some deciduous shrubs to let light through in spring. Each leafy layer has a different clientele; thrushes in the treetops, chaffinches in the shrubs below, and blackbirds scratching in the mulch on the ground. Leave a pile of stones or logs in a secluded corner: many insects and spiders will find homes in the crannies, and perhaps one or two larger creatures too.

A hedge is one of the most valuable habitats you can introduce (see page 9), and a pond (see pages 32–35) is also a great bonus, introducing water-dwelling creatures and plants to the garden and attracting many passing wildlife visitors to drink and bathe.

The plants you grow in the garden can be a useful source of food for wildlife: insects that feed on pollen and nectar, particularly bees, can easily be attracted to visit your flower border (see pages 28–29). Aim to have blooms over as long a period as possible, followed by seeds and berrying shrubs for the birds. Leaf-eating insects are much more selective; they will usually be found in greater numbers on native plants. Hedges and wild-flower meadows (see pages 41–42) are a good way of introducing native plants into a small garden, and woodland wild flowers will grow under deciduous shrubs and trees.

A dry-stone retaining wall has plenty of nooks and crannies: these make ideal homes for a variety of creatures from ground beetles to slow-worms. It also provides a place where plants which appreciate free-draining conditions can grow.

Several garden birds, such as thrushes and robins, find well-tilled beds and a patch of lawn the perfect worm-catching habitat. In contrast, an area of uncut grass provides shelter for other insects and small mammals, and attracts different types of bird.

Many small birds, such as wrens, also make good use of all the tiny hunting-grounds in quiet corners, such as under drainpipes and windowframes, in the corners of cobwebby outhouses where spiders and insects lurk, and around the tangled roots of ivy, honeysuckle and other garden climbers. Spotted flycatchers have been seen nesting in creeper-clad walls and even in hanging baskets, while pied wagtails are at home on flat roofs and gravel.

Garden-dwelling birds love good cover, so allow a bit of undergrowth. They will also appreciate dense shrubs and climbers which can be left undisturbed during the breeding season. To provide them with nest-building material, leave a bit of moss or dead grass in the lawn.

The amount of natural food and shelter you can supply in a small garden is necessarily limited, so artificial extras such as a bird table and nesting boxes can boost the number of birds in a small garden.

Song-thrush.

Robin.

Plants to attract birds

Plants for seeds

Birds such as greenfinches and goldfinches can have a feast from seedheads in autumn, so do not be too hasty to tidy the flower borders.

A number of other plants will be much appreciated by birds for their seeds, so why not grow some of the plants on this page?

Goldenrod flowers provide nectar and pollen for insects late into the autumn, and birds love the seeds.

Centaurea spp. cornflower.

Aster spp. aster.

Some more good plants for seeds:
Dipsacus fullonum teazle
Foeniculum vulgare fennel
Helianthus annuus sunflower
Lavandula spp. lavender
Myosotis spp. forget-me-not
Salvia officinalis sage
Scabiosa spp. scabious

Background picture: Teazle seedheads remain attractive all winter and provide a good feed for greenfinches and goldfinches.

Violas.

Plants for berries

Shrubs which have a good crop of berries will bring in blackbirds, missel-thrushes and other fruit-eaters.

Red and orange berries are usually the most popular, but berries that are left uneaten at first or ripen late are useful when food in the hedgerows becomes scarce.

▲ *Rosa rugosa* – a vigorous shrub of the rose family with pink flowers followed by large rosehips.

▲ *Pyracantha* spp. pyracantha – a useful shrub with white flowers and a generous crop of red, yellow or orange berries.

Other good shrubs to plant would be:
Berberis spp. berberis
Ilex aquifolium holly
Mahonia spp. mahonia
Skimmia japonica skimmia
Symphoricarpus x *doorenbossii* snowberry
Viburnum davidii viburnum
Viburnum opulus guelder rose

▲ The berries of *Cotoneaster horizontalis* bring blackbirds and other fruit-eating birds into the garden; in summer the white flowers will be alive with bees.

▲ *Lonicera* spp. honeysuckle. For another climber, try *Hedera helix* ivy (see page 9).

◀ *Sorbus* spp.

▲ *Malus* varieties crab apple.

Crataegus monogyna (hawthorn), with its red haws, would be another good choice (see page 10).

Plants for butterflies and bees

These insects are always welcome in the garden, the bright colours of the butterflies and the contented hum of bees adding to the atmosphere of summer. Bees are also important pollinators of fruit and vegetable crops. Both insects fly far and wide in search of food, so a sunny flower border will readily attract them.

Butterflies look for nectar-rich summer flowers, and with their long tongues can reach into blooms which are inaccessible to other insects. They also visit many of the flowers that are popular with bees. Getting butterflies to breed in the garden is much more difficult. You have to have the right food plants for the caterpillars, in the right condition and in the right place. However, if you plant a patch of nettles in a really sunny sheltered spot, you might be lucky enough to entice Red Admiral or tortoiseshell butterflies to lay their eggs.

Sedum spectabile, with its rosettes of fleshy evergreen leaves, thrives in hot, dry conditions; the late-summer flowers are a magnet for bees and butterflies, such as this small copper.

Peacock.

Orange tip (above). *Lunaria annua* – honesty (right) – is a good food plant for the caterpillar of this butterfly.

Valeriana officinalis – red valerian – has thin narrow florets which the long-tongued butterflies can reach into for nectar.

Butterflies are drawn to *Buddleia* bushes – the ordinary lilac- and white-flowered ones are better than the newer red or deep-purple varieties.

Holly blue.

Tortoiseshell.

Bees visit flowers for both nectar and pollen, and a continuous food supply from early spring to late autumn is important. Most cottage-garden-type flowers are good for bees, and other particular favourites are herbs of the *Labiatae* family such as thyme, marjoram, mint, lavender and lemon balm. Avoid frilly hybrids as these often have meagre nectar supplies and the multitude of petals can stop insects getting inside.

The bumble bee is a great asset to any garden.

Thymus thyme. This fragrant herb not only attracts bees but also is a wonderful addition to cooking, for stews, salads and many more dishes.

Ivy is valuable for its late-autumn flowers.

Phacelia tanacetifolia phacelia. This produces an attractive blue hazy patch literally buzzing with bees.

Mentha spicata – mint – is always useful in the kitchen.

Origanum vulgare wild marjoram. A good culinary herb and also much loved by bees and butterflies.

Crocuses extend the food season for bees.

More insect friends and the plants they like

Not all the insects in the garden are out to eat your plants! Most are quite innocent and some positively beneficial: pollinating fruit and vegetables and preying on common garden pests. Here are some easily recognisable examples.

Anthocorid bugs prey on aphids, capsid bugs, caterpillars, midges, blossom weevil larvae, scale insects and red spider mites.

The flat umbels of fennel *(Foeniculum vulgare)* make an ideal feeding place for hoverflies, and the aromatic leaves can be used in the kitchen. The plant will tolerate dry conditions, and although it grows to about 1.2m (4ft) it rarely needs staking. Pollen- and nectar-feeding insects also love sunflowers *(Helianthus annuus)*.

Slugs, snails and many insects are the favoured food of centipedes.

Ladybird larvae prey on aphids, mealy-bugs, thrips, spider mites and scale insects...

...and so do ladybirds. To encourage them, do not tidy up too much in autumn: leave some dry plant debris and hollow stems as hibernation sites. Grow a few nettles for nettle aphids, which provide much-needed food for the emerging ladybirds in spring.

Ground beetles eat slugs, root aphids, and carrot and cabbage rootfly eggs and larvae.

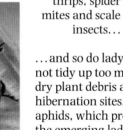

If you are lucky, you may find a glow-worm. They eat slugs and snails.

Hoverfly larvae eat aphids, fruit-tree spider mites, and small caterpillars.

Hoverfly.

Lacewing fly. Their larvae will keep down aphids, leafhoppers, scale insects, and caterpillars.

Plants to attract hoverflies

The best food plants for hoverflies and lacewings are those which have their pollen and nectar easily accessible: single open flowers such as pot marigolds, and flat-headed umbellifers such as dill and fennel. These plants also attract a range of parasitic wasps and flies, all of which help to keep down garden pests.

Calendula officinalis pot marigold.

The self-seeding annual *Limnanthes douglasii* (poached-egg plant) attracts both bees and hoverflies; it is low-growing and could be used to edge either flower or vegetable beds.

Nemophila baby blue eyes is popular with hoverflies.

Eschscholzia spp. Californian poppy.

Some other plants which attract hoverflies are:

Achillea spp. yarrow
Anaphalis spp. pearl everlasting
Chrysanthemum maximum Shasta daisy
Convolvulus tricolor annual convolvulus
Eryngium spp. sea holly
Fragaria vesca wild strawberry
Iberis spp. candytuft

31

Designing and planting your pond

A pond is a great asset to an ecological garden. The bigger it is, the more scope there is for different plants and wildlife, and the more interest it adds to the garden. However, even a small pond can support quite a community of creatures and will attract passing trade from birds, insects and small mammals.

The one essential characteristic for a wildlife pond is that it should have at least one shallow edge – birds cannot bathe in a deep straight-sided pond, and if frogs get in they cannot get out. A depth of 60cm (2ft) or more will guarantee creatures an ice-free place for hibernation.

The best position for a pond is on level ground in a fairly open spot – ideally in sun for at least two-thirds of the day. Avoid very shady places, and choose a site well away from overhanging trees and falling leaves. Try to give wildlife some sheltered access to the pond from the rest of the garden; by putting it at the edge of a flower border, shrubbery, or wild-flower meadow, for example.

Mimulus luteus monkey musk.

Marginal plants for shallow water at the edges of the pond

Floating plants
Leaves floating on the surface should cover about one-third of the water surface: they provide shade for underwater creatures and help prevent algal growth.

Veronica beccabunga brooklime.

Straitiotes aloides water soldier – a free-floating plant.

Iris pseudacorus yellow flag.

Caltha palustris marsh marigold.

Menyanthes trifoliata bog bean.

Stones hold heat for basking dragonflies and gaps between them give amphibians shelter

Have at least one gently sloping side to enable creatures to get in and out easily

Submerged plants
Submerged plants oxygenate the water and are essential to the health of the pond.

Shelves for marginal plants; different plants like to grow in different depths of water

Ceratophyllum demersum hornwort.

The plants suggested here are suitable for a small garden pond around 2 x 1.2m (6 x 4ft) in surface area and 45cm (18in) deep.

A sheet liner will enable you to create any shape of pond; butyl is generally more expensive than plastic or PVC, but lasts longer.

If you have young children, you may want to avoid open water in the garden but you can still provide for wildlife. Create a small marshy area, for example, by lining a hole as for a pond, but filling it with soil: as this cannot drain it is easy to keep it constantly water-logged. A small bubbler fountain coming up through pebbles will allow creatures to drink and bathe.

The pond is one place where you do not want rich soil: nutrients in the water encourage the growth of algae. If anything, it is best to place a thin layer of subsoil or gravel on the pond bottom. Silt will gradu-ally accumulate. Put new plants in purpose-made pond baskets or 'planting crates' lined with a porous material such as hessian or polypropylene sheeting.

Plants for a marshy area
(where soil is kept permanently wet)

Ajuga reptans bugle.

Cardamine pratensis lady's smock.

Lysimachia nummularia creeping Jenny.

Lychnis flos-cuculi ragged robin.

Nymphoides peltata fringed waterlily. This has floating leaves but is anchored to the bottom of the pond.

Iris pseudacorus yellow flag.

Hottonia palustris water violet.

Liner raised in hump to retain soil in marsh

Marshy area filled with soil for bog plants

Planting crate with lattice sides to let water in and eventually let roots out

Sheet liner

An underlay of old carpet, newspaper, or sand stops stones puncturing the liner

Plants are important to the health of a pond. Choose a mixture of floating, marginal, and submerged plants, as each has a different role to play. Algae may turn the water in the pond to 'pea soup' a few weeks after you fill it, but this should clear once plants establish and start using up nutrients. Do not be tempted to change the water – you will only make matters worse.

Pond wildlife

You will be surprised at the amount of wildlife that will appear almost overnight in a new pond, even if you fill it with tap water. However, the best way to introduce a wide variety of creatures quickly is to add a bucketful of water from a neighbour's pond. You could also add some frogspawn in spring. It is better not to introduce goldfish, as they eat frogspawn and tadpoles.

If you do not know anyone with a pond, you could contact your local wildlife trust.

Native water plants are relatively easy to buy from pond-plant specialists and even at some garden centres. Beware, however, as many commonly sold species of both native and exotic plants would easily take over a small pond. Avoid the most rampant – Canadian pondweed (*Elodea canadensis*), for example – and restrict others by growing them in planting crates.

Adapting existing ponds for wildlife

• If your pond has steep sides, create a gentle slope at one end with rocks and gravel.

• Raised ponds need a similar access ramp on the outside.

• If the pond is completely surrounded by lawn or paving, remove a small area to create a marsh, rock garden or wild-flower patch which will give shelter to wildlife.

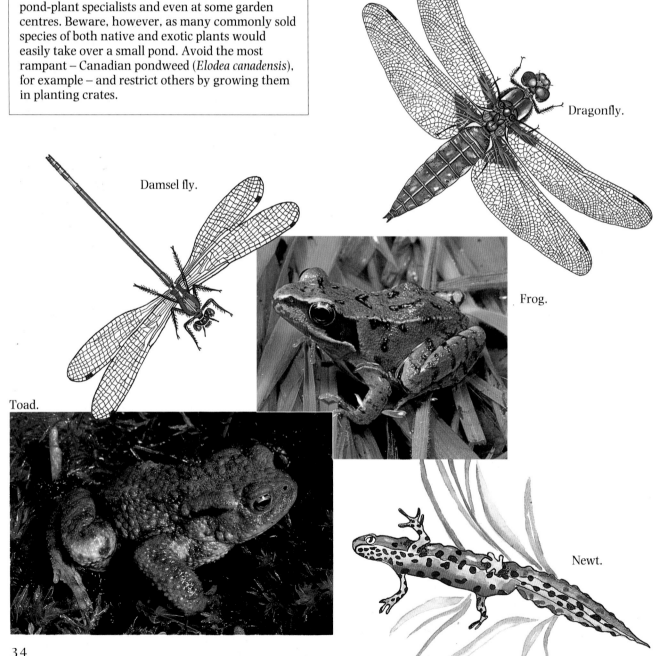

Dragonfly.

Damsel fly.

Frog.

Toad.

Newt.

These ponds are only about 1m (3ft) across, yet they have their own busy population of water insects, visiting damsel flies, and a handsome frog which takes up summer residence.

The flower border next to this pond gives sheltered access for timid creatures, while the lawn provides an open place for birds to bathe – and for you to watch their antics.

This wilder pond is planted only with native water and marsh plants.

Annuals, *e.g.* groundsel (above), chickweed.

Perennials with stems creeping over the ground, *e.g.* creeping buttercup (above), cinquefoil.

Perennials with tap roots, *e.g.* dandelions (above), docks.

Weeds

Only by identifying the weeds you have in the garden can you determine the problem they pose and how to deal with it. Some of the sorts of weeds you might find, in roughly increasing order of trouble, are shown in the pictures above.

Living with your weeds

Not all weeds are necessarily bad. Many provide food for wildlife, and some are attractive in their own right. At the very least, weeds make good compost material. As long as they are not out of control or competing with garden plants, they can have a part to play in the garden.

Conversely, some ornamental plants can get out of hand and become weeds. For example, Rose of Sharon (*Hypericum calycinum*), common snowberry (*Symphoricarpus albus*), and even bluebells can be a problem if you are taking over a neglected garden. Tolerate weeds where appropriate – nettles on a patch by the compost heap for example – but keep them under control and cut them down before they seed.

To clear unplanted ground of weeds, try covering it with flattened cardboard cartons weighted with pieces of old wood.

Clearing the ground

Perennial weeds are very difficult to control once they are amongst established plants, so by clearing an area thoroughly before planting you can prevent serious problems. Sometimes there is no alternative but to give an existing bed the same treatment: you may need to lift all the plants in a herbaceous border temporarily. The following methods can all be used to clear weeds:

Perennials with a relatively shallow network of creeping roots, *e.g.* couch grass (above), ground elder.

Perennials with deep, branching roots, *e.g.* bindweed (above), creeping thistle.

Perennials with corms or bulbils, *e.g.* celandine (above), bulbous buttercup, oxalis.

Digging in This is most suitable for small areas containing annuals and shallow-rooted perennials. Perennial weeds must be buried at least 15cm (6in) down if they are not to regrow. Do not mix topsoil with subsoil. Digging in is hard work, particularly on heavy land, but gives immediate results; it is not effective for very deep-rooted perennials.

Forking and hand-weeding This is another option for similar areas. You can fork or hand-weed at any time of year if soil conditions are suitable. It is easiest on light land. Planting can take place immediately provided that the job was thorough.

Weeding with a hand fork.

Mulching If you exclude light from weeds while they are trying to grow, they will gradually become exhausted and die. This is an effective way to clear annuals and perennials from any area. Suitable light-excluding materials include hessian-backed wool carpet, cardboard, and black plastic.

The time it takes to clear the weeds depends on what type they are. Annual weeds can be cleared in a month or two, and shallow-rooted perennials will be largely eliminated over six to eight months, but this must be during the growing season (March to October). Deep-rooted perennials may take two years or more to die off properly.

You need not necessarily lose growing time when you are clearing ground between widely spaced plants – you can put mulches around them, or, in some cases, plant through a mulch put down on prepared ground.

Using mulches

As well as being good for clearing weedy areas, mulches can be used regularly instead of hoeing or hand weeding to control seasonal weed growth. The type of mulch to use depends on the weeds present and what you are growing – use biodegradable mulches, not plastics, wherever possible. There are some examples on the next page.

Straw mulch under roses.

Bark used as a mulch for irises.

A mulch of wood-chips.

Gravel mulch.

Shrubs   Use shreddings, bark, woodchips, hay or straw around shrubs. A thick layer of newspaper hidden underneath will help to clear established perennial weeds. On a new bed, you could plant through a porous polypropylene membrane and disguise it in a similar way.

Herbaceous borders   Clear the beds thoroughly before planting, then use biodegradable mulches. Those such as leaf-mould or fine bark which break down fairly readily are best, as the mulch often becomes incorporated into the soil when plants are lifted and divided.

Rockeries and alpine banks   Thoroughly clear weedy ground before planting. Afterwards, mulch with fine-grade bark or gravel. Alternatively, plant through a porous membrane.

Trees in rough grass   Use a 1 x 1m (3 x 3ft) mulching mat around the tree until it is established; this can be made of wool matting, cardboard covered with straw, or thick black plastic.

Hedges   On weedy ground, surround hedging plants with newspaper weighted with hay, straw, or grass mowings. Alternatively, plant small hedging plants through a strip of black plastic and disguise it with shreddings.

Making paths

Give all permanent hard paths good foundations, so perennial weeds cannot penetrate and seedlings cannot become established. A polypropylene membrane can help by stopping the path materials mixing with the soil. Good retaining edges are essential for paths with a loose surface. For temporary or informal paths, use strips of old hessian-backed carpet covered in bark, woodchips, or shredded prunings.

A mulch of spent organic mushroom compost.

Hebe growing through a grass mulch.

Lawns and wild flowers

Lawns

There is really no substitute for a lawn when it comes to having a picnic or playing games. Lawns also have their own wildlife community, as they contain various grasses, 'weeds' and all the creatures associated with them.

A lawn does not have to be totally grass. Some wild meadow plants will withstand mowing and trampling and still remain green – often in situations when grass will not. Good examples are yarrow, bird's-foot trefoil, clover and daisies. Their leaves add varied shapes and textures to the lawn, and provided that you keep conditions as close as possible to the ideal for lawn grasses, these 'weeds' should not become dominant. Many other weeds will simply disappear once you have begun to mow the lawn regularly, as they are not adapted to constant cutting.

Those that do need clearing, both on new sites and existing lawns, are the perennials with flat spreading leaves such as dandelions and plantains: these avoid the mower and also shade out the grass.

Clover is a desirable plant to have in the lawn as it adds nitrogen to the soil and feeds the grass. You can add seed of wild white clover to your lawn seed, or scatter it into an existing lawn where clover does not occur naturally.

Grass mixtures   When creating a new lawn, it is important to have a fairly sunny, well-drained site and to choose the right kind of grass mixture. Seed companies usually supply:

• 'wear-tolerant' mixtures; these contain coarser grasses such as perennial rye grass which stand rough use and regrow quickly if damaged.

• 'ornamental' or 'high-quality' mixtures; these contain fine grasses which grow less vigorously and cut cleanly, giving a velvety green sward.

• 'general-purpose' mixtures between these extremes.

• 'shade-tolerant' mixtures able to flourish in low light.

There is usually less choice of grass mixtures if you are using turf, but you should have the option of hard-wearing or ornamental turf from most suppliers. 'Meadow turf' will contain coarse agricultural grasses and probably some meadow weeds. It will need frequent mowing to keep it short, but may be quite suitable for some situations.

Maintenance   The key to maintaining a healthy, relatively weed-free lawn is correct mowing. This will encourage the growth of lawn grasses at the expense of weeds and other grass species:

• Do not mow too low: a cutting height of 2.5cm (1in) is about right for a general-purpose lawn.

• Mow every time the grass gets about half as tall again (*i.e.* 3.75cm (1½in) for a general-purpose lawn); thus you will not necessarily mow once a week, but sometimes more and sometimes less often.

• Leave the mowings on the lawn at nearly every mowing to return the fertility, but not when the grass has got too long or in cold wet conditions when the mowings would lie about in clumps on the surface.

Herb lawns
If you have only a small area of lawn, a herb lawn makes a lovely feature. Not intended for heavy wear, a herb lawn is nonetheless capable of being walked upon, is wonderfully fragrant when bruised, and needs  no mowing! The plants are naturally prostrate: try thyme, or camomile (shown here).

Wild flowers

Flowers for areas under trees   Grass does not grow well under trees because of the lack of light, water and nutrients. However, some spring wild flowers, such as primroses and snowdrops, which bloom before the leaf canopy forms, do well under deciduous trees. As they bloom early, the area can be cut in early summer. Always wait until at least six weeks after bulbs have finished flowering before cutting: this allows time for the leaves to feed the bulbs for next year's blooms. An alternative is not to cut until autumn, so you can grow later-flowering woodland plants such as foxgloves and campion.

Very few plants will grow under conifers because it is so dark and dry all year round. Let the branches grow down to the ground to provide cover for wildlife.

Woodland wild flowers

1. *Endymion* bluebell (flowers May).

2. *Primula vulgaris* primrose (flowers March–May).

3. *Galanthus nivalis* snowdrop (flowers January–March).

4. *Digitalis purpurea* foxglove (flowers June–September). The leaves of foxgloves are poisonous.

5. *Polygonatum multiflorum* Solomon's seal (flowers May–June).

6. *Viola* violet (flowers March–May).

7. *Anemone nemorosa* wood anemone (flowers March–May).

8. *Silene dioica* red campion (flowers June–September).

1

2

3

4

Meadow wild flowers

1. *Primula veris* cowslip (suitable for chalky soil; flowers April–May).

2. *Leucanthemum vulgare* ox-eye daisy (most soils; flowers May–August).

3. *Galium verum* lady's bedstraw (most well-drained soil; flowers July–August).

4. *Centaurea scabiosa* greater knapweed (alkaline soil preferred; flowers June–August).

5. *Anthyllis vulneria* kidney vetch (most well-drained soil; flowers April–September).

6. *Lotus corniculatus* bird's-foot trefoil (light soil – chalk preferred; flowers May–September).

7. *Knautia arvensis* field scabious (most soils; flowers July–September).

8. *Medicago lupilina* black medick (most well-drained soil; flowers April–October).

5

6

7

8

Wild-flower meadow 'patches'

A patch of long grass with naturalised flowers can be more appropriate than a lawn in some areas. It gives you the opportunity to grow native meadow plants, provides an extra habitat for wildlife – and does not need mowing every week!

Meadow wild flowers need a *low* soil fertility – quite the opposite to most garden plants. This restricts the growth of vigorous grasses and enables the wild flowers to compete. The ideal way to create a wild-flower patch is to remove any turf and topsoil from the site and replace it with subsoil. Also clear the site of any perennial weeds.

Choose a selection of wild flowers and fine grasses suitable for your soil type and pH. Several seed companies sell ready-made mixtures, some of which are collected from natural meadows. The flowers should bloom over roughly the same period, either all in spring or all in summer, so that you can establish a cutting régime (see below).

Early September to mid October is the best time to sow, as some species need a cold period before they will germinate. You can always add to the patch later with bulbs or plants raised in pots.

To maintain your patch, a twice-yearly cut with shears, sickle or strimmer should be sufficient, although wild-flower patches in lawns can be mown with the rest of the lawn for some of the year. Always let the flowers set at least some seed, and remove the 'hay' and mowings to keep the fertility low.

• Spring-flowering meadow – cut late June/early July, then mow until autumn or cut again in November.

• Summer-flowering meadow – cut in late spring (or mow up until then, with the mower blades set to give a high cut), and then cut again in November.

Creating a wild-flower patch in an existing lawn

As long as you have not used weedkiller in recent years, your lawn probably contains some wild flowers. Leave a patch to grow long until June or July to see what blooms. Then cut it as described above, always removing the 'hay' and mowings. Add to the patch in spring or autumn with wild flowers raised in pots.

Cornfield flowers

The old cornfield weeds such as corn cockle (inset), corn marigolds, cornflowers and poppies (main picture) have almost been eradicated by intensive farming methods, but you can enjoy them in your own garden. A sunny flower border is ideal for growing them. Sow the seed in autumn, and it should produce a brilliant patch of colourful blooms the following summer. Allow the flowers to seed, then lightly fork the ground to produce a seedbed for the fallen seed, and remove any garden weeds.

Note: the seeds of corn cockle are poisonous.

Good ecological gardening

The techniques you use in the garden and the plants and products you buy can have effects far beyond the garden fence. Ecological gardeners recognise this and try to minimise pollution and environmental damage not only on their own small plots but also in the world outside.

This is not always easy or obvious. Our knowledge is limited and there are many grey areas. Compromises have to be made. This chapter offers guidelines on a few issues, which should at least make you aware of the wider implications of your gardening.

Avoiding bonfires

The traditional garden bonfire not only destroys organic matter valuable to the health of the soil but also pollutes the air with smoke. It is far better to compost green materials, shred woody prunings and make your fallen leaves into leaf-mould (see page 18). Larger branches can be cut up and left in an out-of-the-way corner for the benefit of wildlife (see page 24). If you do find you have more material than you can cope with, find out whether your local authority has a site where garden waste is separately collected and composted. If not, ask why not!

If a bonfire is really necessary – to destroy diseased wood, for example – minimise smoke by making sure that the material is dry and that there is a slight wind to fan the flames.

Using plastics

Plastics use up oil when they are manufactured and cause pollution when they are disposed of, so keep their use in the garden to a minimum. They are most acceptable in situations where they will have a long life – plastic or polypropylene sheets under paths to prevent weeds growing, for example. If you need them for short-term mulches – in ground clearance or around annuals – use heavy grades of material that can be removed without tearing and then reused. Many plastics can be recycled, and some local authorities have collection points for old plastic. If you are buying plastic products such as compost bins, look out for those made of recycled material. You may also be able to 'recycle' some discarded household plastics in the garden. Yoghurt cartons can be used as pots, for example (pierce holes for drainage) and lemonade bottles with the bottoms cut off make good individual cloches for young plants.

Do not burn your fallen leaves or garden rubbish!

Reuse plastic yoghurt cartons for growing seedlings.

Empty plastic lemonade bottles make good mini-greenhouses for young plants.

Conserving water

Water should not be treated as a throw-away product, but as a valuable natural resource. By digging in organic matter and using mulches (see pages 37–38), you will already be helping your garden to retain moisture. You can also reduce the need to water by choosing drought-resistant plants for dry areas (see page 21). However, some watering will nearly always be necessary, especially for new plants and vegetable crops.

A watering can or seep hose usually applies water more efficiently than a sprinkler. Water is directed exactly where you want it – at the plant roots – rather than being wasted on bare ground or paths, or lost by evaporation. To minimise the use of mains water, save rainwater from roofs by fitting diverters to downpipes. These will channel the water into butts for storage.

During periods of drought, waste water from the house can also be valuable. However, it should be used with care as it may contain products damaging to plants. Avoid using water containing a high concentration of bleaches or detergents, such as that from the wash cycle of the washing machine. Substances found in some household cleaners – particularly boron – can also be harmful.

Simple soaps are the safest, but even these tend to make the soil alkaline, so do not use soapy water on acid-loving plants. Also avoid using it continually on the same small area of garden, or for plants in containers.

There should be no danger to human health, particularly if the water is used straight away and not stored. However, it is sensible to use the dirtiest water on ornamental crops and only the cleanest on fruit and vegetables, avoiding crops to be eaten raw.

Timber and its treatment

Check the source of any timber that you buy for use in the garden to make sure that it comes from local and/or sustainably managed plantations. Conifers (such as larch, pine and spruce) grown in Europe and British-grown hardwoods usually come into these categories – they may be marked with a symbol to denote it. Avoid using tropical hardwoods or any other timber that may be contributing to loss of natural woodland.

Fence-posts and panels and other products sold for use in the garden are often treated with anti-rotting chemicals to increase their resistence to attack by bacteria and fungi, and repeat preservative treatments are often recommended by manufacturers. To avoid using these chemicals, you could use untreated wood and

• accept that it will not last so long. Reuse old wood where possible to reduce costs: *e.g.* compost bins can be made from old pallets;

• avoid contact between the wood, air and soil where possible, as this is the point where it is most susceptible to decay. For example, use concrete bases for fence posts; stand cold frames and benches on bricks; line planters and compost bins with old pieces of thick plastic sheeting;

• try treating the wood with one of the 'natural' wood preservatives on the market. These are made from materials such as vegetable oils and tree resins.

A traditional wooden water-butt.

Bath-water diverter.

Drainpipe rainwater diverter.

Fine bark   Compost   Animal manure   Mushroom compost

Leaf-mould   Spent hops   Cocoa shell   Coir dust

Some alternatives to peat.

Alternatives to peat

The extraction of peat threatens valuable wildlife habitats. Although it is often recommended for improving soils, especially when trees and shrubs are planted, there are now better products available.

The best are those that are both organic and locally produced – compost and leaf-mould from your own garden, for example. Alternatively, use products such as farmyard or stable manure (see page 18), or branded planting mixtures containing materials such as composted bark, wood fibre, or brewers' waste. Apart from being ecologically more acceptable, these contribute far more to the soil life than a sterile substance such as peat.

The same principles apply to seed and potting mixtures. Wherever possible, buy ones which have a recognised organic symbol, and avoid those containing peat or imported products. Leaf-mould is the best home-made substitute for peat in such mixtures.

Threatened plant species

Gardeners can unwittingly contribute to the loss of plants in their natural habitats. Victorian plant-collectors, for example, were so keen to acquire the Royal fern – a British native – that it is now rare in the wild, and some wild flowers are under a similar threat today.

Wild orchids have become increasingly rare.

It is illegal to dig up any wild plants from the countryside, or from private land unless you have permission from the owner. It is even illegal to collect seed from certain rare species. When buying wild plants, choose from companies which state that their seeds and plants are raised by growers, but come originally from native stock. Ideally, buy from local nurseries using locally produced seed and plants.

Trade in bulbs dug from the wild is also threatening their natural existence in countries such as Turkey and Portugal. Snowdrops, aconites and cyclamen are familar examples of plants under threat. Only buy from companies which state that their bulbs are grown from cultivated stock.

Loss of wild plant species and old cultivated varities of fruit, vegetables and flowers means that important genetic material is being lost forever. This could have serious consequences for plant breeders in the future.

Pesticides

As the previous chapters have shown, the ecological gardener encourages plants to be healthy by giving them the right conditions, feeding the soil with organic matter, and encouraging an environment where pests are likely to be controlled by natural predators. However, it would be foolish to suggest that problems never arise and that there is nothing you can do if your favourite plant is looking sickly or being devastated by an unexpected pest attack.

The main problem with most pesticides is that they kill not only the pests but also many harmless creatures, many of which are actually predators of other pests. Pesticides also persist in the environment, taking their toll long after the spray has been applied. Once you start using pesticides, problems in the garden are quite likely to get worse.

In contrast to a kill-all spray, the ecological answers to pests and diseases are usually specific to each particular problem. You need to find something out about the 'ecology' of the pest or disease – its habits and lifecycle – so that you can take the right action at the right time, such as using a physical barrier to deter a pest, putting out a trap, or pruning out diseased stems. Details of these measures are beyond the scope of this book, but there are many that can help you.

As a very last resort, there are a few non-persistent sprays that could be used. For example, insecticidal soap, which is made from soaps of vegetable origin, could be used for spot-spraying a bad attack of aphids. Although these sprays break down rapidly once applied, they can still harm beneficial creatures which are directly hit and they should never be used on a regular basis.

Glossary

Annual: a plant which grows from seed, flowers, sets seed, and dies during one year.

Brandlings: small red worms which live in and feed on piles of decaying organic matter. They carry out the composting process in worm bins.

Bulbils: small bulb-like organs which form at the base of the leaves of a plant or in place of flowers, and break off to form new plants.

Compost activator: a substance used to speed up the composting process.

Corm: a type of underground swollen stem, used by the plant as a storage organ.

Dry-stone wall: wall in which the stones are put together without any cement or mortar.

Herbaceous plant: a non-woody perennial plant with leafy growth which dies back in winter.

Leaching: the washing-out of plant nutrients.

Microclimate: a local variation in climatic factors such as temperature, wind, and humidity, such as can occur within a garden.

Mulch: any material spread over the soil.

Organic: a method of growing plants which avoids the use of chemical pesticides and artificial fertilisers.

Organic matter: any bulky material of animal or vegetable origin.

Plant nutrient: any of the mineral substances that are absorbed by the roots of plants for nourishment.

Spp.: abbreviation for species.

Umbellifers: plants belonging to the family *Umbelliferae*, characterised by flat umbrella-like flowerheads or umbels.

Bibliography

Pears, Pauline, *Beds: labour-saving, space-saving, more productive gardening* (1992) HDRA/Search Press.

Pears, Pauline, *Healthy Fruit and Vegetables: how to avoid diseases, disorders and deficiencies* (1991) HDRA/Search Press.

Pears, Pauline, *How to Make your Garden Fertile: all about compost* (1991) HDRA/Search Press.

Pears, Pauline, and Sherman, Bob, *Pests: how to control them on fruit and vegetables* (1992) HDRA/Search Press.

Readman, Jo, *Muck and Magic* (1993) HDRA/Search Press.

Readman, Jo, *Soil Care and Management* (1991) HDRA/Search Press.

Readman, Jo, *Weeds: how to control and love them* (1991) HDRA/Search Press.

Index